BASEBALL LEGENDS ALPHABET

Words by Robin Feiner

A is for Hank Aaron.
This record-setting All-Star and three-time Gold Glove recipient played 21 seasons for the Braves. In an event that polarized America, 'Hammerin' Hank' beat Babe Ruth's sacred home run record, and held the new record for 33 years.
What a legend!

B is for Yogi **B**erra. This legendary Yankee is an 18-time All-Star and record 10-time World Series champion. He caught the only perfect game in World Series history, and the image of him leaping into Don Larsen's arms after the final out is one of the most iconic images in sports history!

C is for Roberto **C**lemente. His career was filled with highlights, including being named World Series MVP in 1971, but this Puerto Rican's legacy lives on beyond the diamond. A beloved humanitarian until the end, he lived to help others and promote equality for all. The Roberto Clemente Award is given every year in his honor.

Dd

D is for Joe **Di**Maggio. 'Joltin' Joe' played his entire 13-year major league career with the Yankees, winning nine World Series and three MVP awards. One of the greatest players of all time, he's remembered for his 56-game hitting streak, and marriage to Marilyn Monroe.

E is for **E**rnie Banks. Named in the Major League Baseball All-Century Team, there is no doubt 'Mr. Cub' is one of the all-time greats. A shortstop for the Cubs, he became their first ever Gold Glove winner. This legend was also awarded the Presidential Medal of Freedom.

Ff

F is for **F**rank Robinson.
This 14-time All-Star became
the only player to win league
MVP honors in both the National
and American Leagues. He was
also the first African-American
manager in the majors – truly
one of the greats.

Gg

G is for **G**reg Maddux.
This legendary pitcher was
the first to win the Cy Young
Award four times in a row
(1992–1995). He also holds
the record for most Gold Glove
awards (18), and is still the
only pitcher to have won at
least 15 games for 17 straight
seasons!

PIRATES

**H is for Honus Wagner.
As a shortstop, this all-rounder
was a five-time stolen base
leader, with a career total of
723 steals! 'The Flying Dutch-
man' joined fellow greats Babe
Ruth and Ty Cobb as one of the
first ever players to be inducted
into the Baseball Hall of Fame.**

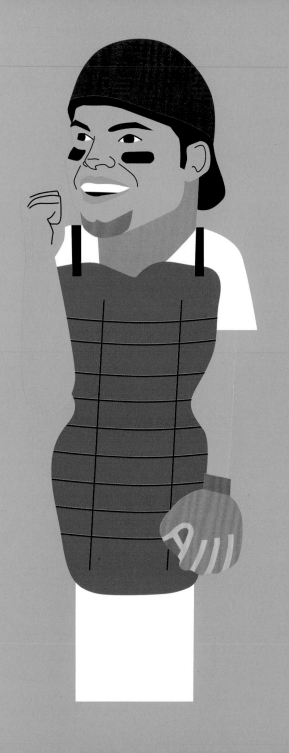

I is for Iván Rodríguez. Winning the Gold Glove Award 13 times, 'Pudge' is one of the best defensive catchers to ever play the game. During his career, he had the best caught stealing percentage of any catcher in Major League Baseball. What a legend!

Jj

J is for Jackie Robinson. Literally changing the face of baseball, Robinson broke Major League Baseball's color barrier when he debuted for the Brooklyn Dodgers in 1947, and went on to become the first African-American to be inducted into the Baseball Hall of Fame.

K is for **K**en Griffey Jr. As the namesake of his All-Star father, 'The Kid' became a 13-time All-Star himself and earned his place in the Baseball Hall of Fame. The legendary father and son duo were the first ever to play for the same team in the same game.

L is for Lou Gehrig. Considered the greatest first baseman of all time, 'The Iron Horse' sadly died of amyotrophic lateral sclerosis, which became known as Lou Gehrig's disease. It was the first time a major league team retired a uniform number in a player's honor.

Mm

M is for Mickey **M**antle.
This three-time MVP, 20-time
All-Star and Triple Crown
winner was considered by
many as the greatest switch-
hitter in baseball history.
'The Mick' smashed a total
of 536 home runs, despite
being plagued with bone
disease for most of his career.

N is for Nolan Ryan.
With his pitches consistently clocking over 100 miles an hour, they didn't call him 'The Ryan Express' for nothing! During his record 27-year career, he set (and still holds) the record for most strikeouts (5,714) and most walks (2,795). Legendary!

Oo

O is for Mel **O**tt.
Being shorter than most power-hitters, this New York Giant used an unconventional batting style to make an impact. 'Master Melvin' holds the record for being the youngest player to hit 100 home runs, and the first National Leaguer to hit 500 home runs. What a legend!

P is for Satchel **P**aige. Initially barred from the major leagues because he was African-American, Paige became its oldest rookie at 42 years of age. He also made history as the first Negro Leagues player to pitch in the World Series. His showmanship will never be forgotten.

BOSTON

Q is for Joe **Q**uinn.
The first ever Australian-born player to hit the major leagues, Quinn was a defensive second baseman for 17 seasons in MLB. Off the field, he advocated for players' rights, and was The Sporting News' "most popular player in baseball" in 1893.

R is for Babe **R**uth.
With a career total of 714 home runs, and multiple batting and pitching records, no one has ever come close to the legend of 'The Great Bambino'. He transcended sport to become not only a superstar of baseball, but also an iconic figure in American history.

S is for **S**tan Musial.
'Stan the Man' was one
of the most consistent hitters
of all time. This legend played
24 All-Star games. The seven-
time batting champion's statue
stands proudly in his signature
stance in his beloved St. Louis.

Tt

T is for Ted Williams.
A 19-time All-Star, 'Teddy
Ballgame' is considered among
the greatest players to ever
grace the field. He was also
acknowledged for his military
heroism, putting his career
on hold to serve in WWII
and Korea.

Uu

U is for Bob **U**ecker.
With a World Series
championship under his belt,
Uecker retired from MLB
and found his true calling as
a baseball commentator. Since
1971 he's been broadcasting
with passion and humor,
earning him the Baseball Hall
of Fame's Ford C. Frick Award.
"Get up! Get up! Get outta
here! Gone!"

V is for **V**ladimir Guerrero. This Dominican-born powerhouse was the personification of grit and passion. Whether he was fielding or hitting, this right fielder and designated hitter unleashed on every ball. His mighty batting style made him one of the most feared hitters in the game!

W is for **W**illie Mays. With all-round prowess and stats to last a lifetime, 'The Say Hey Kid' is regarded the finest five-tool player of all time. In appreciation of his record-tying 12 Gold Glove awards for an outfielder and 24 All-Star appearances, Ted Williams said, "They invented the All-Star Game for Willie Mays."

Xx

X is for Jimmie Foxx.
Making his MLB debut in 1925,
the three-time MVP was one
of the most feared sluggers of
his era. Becoming the second
player in history (after Babe
Ruth) to hit 500 career home
runs, 'The Beast' was once
described as having "muscles
in his hair."

Y is for Cy Young.
Pitching the first perfect game of the 20th Century, Young set records for most wins, innings pitched and complete games. In his honor, the top pitcher from each league is awarded the Cy Young Award every year. Now that's a lasting legacy!

TIME

Zz

Z is for Dizzy Dean.
This eccentric pitcher led the St. Louis Cardinals to a World Series victory in 1934, and was the last National League pitcher to win 30 games in one season. He later found fame behind the 'mic' as a sports commentator, where his colorful personality really shone!

The ever-expanding legendary library

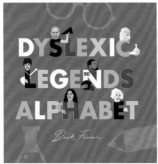   

EXPLORE THESE LEGENDARY ALPHABETS & MORE AT WWW.ALPHABETLEGENDS.COM

BASEBALL LEGENDS ALPHABET
www.alphabetlegends.com

Published by Alphabet Legends Pty Ltd in 2019
Created by Beck Feiner
Copyright © Alphabet Legends Pty Ltd 2019

Printed and bound in China.

9 780648 506348

ALPHABET LEGENDS